NEW JERSEY

NEW YORK
PENNSYLVANIA
NEW JERSEY
DELAWARE
ATLANTIC
OCEAN
NEW YORK CITY
Delaware River
Hudson River
Greenwood Lake
Wanaque Res.
Lake Hopatcong
Musconetcong R.
Passaic R.
Round Valley Res.
Raritan R.
Lower Bay
Toms R.
Rnancocas R.
Barnegat Bay
Mullica R.
Great Egg Harbor R.
Mannington Meadow
Maurice R.
Great Bay
Great Egg Harbor
Delaware Bay
Newton
Paterson
Hackensack
Clifton
Passaic
East Orange
Union City
Belvidere
Morristown
Newark
Jersey City
Phillipsburg
Elizabeth
Bayonne
Somerville
Woodbridge
Edison
Flemington
New Brunswick
Hamilton
TRENTON
Freehold
Lakewood
Brick
Mount Holly
Toms River
Camden
Cherry Hill
Woodbury
Pennsville
Glassboro
Hammonton
Salem
Mays Landing
Vineland
Millville
Bridgeton
Atlantic City
Ocean City
Wildwood
Cape May
287
80
280
95
78
195
295

NEW JERSEY

THE GARDEN STATE

Michael Worek

FIREFLY BOOKS

A Firefly Book

Published by Firefly Books Ltd. 2025

First printing

Library of Congress Control Number: 2024947835

Library and Archives Canada Cataloguing in Publication
Title: New Jersey : the Garden State / Michael Worek.
Names: Worek, Michael, author
Description: Includes index.
Identifiers: Canadiana 20240494245 | ISBN 9780228105466 (hardcover)
Subjects: LCSH: New Jersey—Guidebooks. | LCSH: New Jersey—Description and travel. | LCGFT: Guidebooks.
Classification: LCC F132.3 .W67 2025 | DDC 917.4904/44—dc23

Published in Canada by
Firefly Books Ltd.
50 Staples Avenue, Unit 1
Richmond Hill, Ontario
L4B 0A7

Published in the United States by
Firefly Books (U.S.) Inc.
P.O. Box 1338, Ellicott Station
Buffalo, New York
14205

Cover and interior design: Jacqueline Hope Raynor
Photo Editor: Cathy Hoshino

Printed in China | E

MIX
Paper | Supporting responsible forestry
FSC® C160794
FSC www.fsc.org

INTRODUCTION

New Jersey is the most densely populated state in the Union with some 9,200,000 people living in 7,300 square miles. Originally settled by the Dutch in the early 1600s, Holland ceded the land to Britain in 1664. One of the original 13 colonies, the state supported the American Revolution and was the site of several major battles.

New Jersey was the site of early industrial developments thanks to its abundance of natural resources. Thomas Edison's research and manufacturing complex at West Orange attracted many other industries to the state and New Jersey was a major industrial center well into the 20th century.

Notable places in the state include:

- Princeton University: one of the top academic universities in the country, it also offers a beautiful campus, an international student body and a rich tradition.
- Newark and Jersey City: sophisticated cities with a wide variety of economic opportunities along with a vibrant cultural scene.
- Atlantic City: one of the premier resort destinations in the country with beautiful beaches, an exciting boardwalk and world-class hotels and casinos. Ocean City, Wildwood and Cape May also provide the visitor with more beautiful beaches, sun, sand and entertainment.
- The historic state capital at Trenton abounds in architecture, monuments and museums that preserve and celebrate the rich history of the state.
- The Pine Barrens, in southern New Jersey, preserve an endangered and unique ecosystem while offering visitors the opportunity to experience the solitude of nature.

New Jersey continues to offer something for everybody, visitor and resident alike.

The New Jersey State House in Trenton, originally constructed in 1792, is one of the oldest State Houses still in continuous use in the United States. The design consists of two parallel wings connected by a rotunda (above) with a classically designed dome on the top. The building was almost destroyed by fire in 1885. It was rebuilt after the fire and substantially renovated in 1987 and again in 2017. Today the State House is not only the center of state government but also a local landmark and tourist destination.

Atlantic City's casinos and hotels dominate the skyline as the lights come on at dusk. Gambling was legalized here in 1976 and in 1977 the New Jersey Casino Control Act was signed into law, but Atlantic City has been a popular resort area since the first boardwalk opened in 1870. Today the city receives more than 27 million visitors a year.

(Previous page) The Delaware Water Gap cuts through the Appalachian Mountains just where New Jersey and Pennsylvania meet. The early settlers used the gap to get around the mountains and settle the interior of the state. Interstate 80 now passes through the gap on the New Jersey side and the Delaware River flows through the gap on its way to the Atlantic Ocean at Cape May.

(Above) The 1,100-foot-long Hainesburg Viaduct spans the Paulinskill River in Knowlton Township. When it was completed in 1910, the viaduct was the longest reinforced concrete structure in the world. No longer in use, the last train crossed the viaduct in 1978 and the railway tracks were removed in 1984. The viaduct is still famous for its maze of internal chambers that were once used to inspect the condition of the structure when it was in use.

Buttermilk Falls in the Delaware Water Gap National Recreation Area, one of the highest and most beautiful waterfalls in New Jersey, drops more than 80 feet. A trail accessible at the top of the falls connects with the Appalachian National Scenic Trail which offers specular views of the area around the falls.

The tiny borough of Belmar is less than two square miles in area but its proximity to New York City and Philadelphia makes it a popular holiday destination. In addition to the fishing pier (above), the boardwalk and wide beaches attract large crowds on any warm summer day.

(Left) The lighthouse in Sandy Hook, built in 1764, is the oldest working lighthouse in the United States and is maintained by the United States Coast Guard. Located on the grounds of Fort Hancock in the Gateway National Recreation Area, the lighthouse is open for tours during the summer months.

(Previous page) A fully loaded container ship passes under the Bayonne Bridge on route to Newark Harbor. In 2017, the bridge was raised 64 feet to a height of 215 feet above the Kill Van Kull tidal strait, allowing huge ships to pass underneath. It is the sixth longest steel arch span in the world.

Steel Pier Amusement Park on the Atlantic City Boardwalk originally opened in 1898. At its peak, the pier stretched over 2,000 feet into the ocean but fire destroyed most of the pier in 1982. The current pier is 1,000 feet long and was rebuilt in steel and concrete in 1992. A new 227-foot-tall Ferris wheel (right) was added in 2017. The pier has over 20 rides, including the popular carousel (above), a helicopter station, an arcade, food stands, and stores.

Scarborough Covered Bridge, despite its historic look, was built in 1959 and renovated to modern standards in 1993. It is still a working bridge, carrying traffic in the Barclay Farm neighborhood of Cherry Hill.

(Left) The four-story Red Mill on the Raritan River in Clinton was built in 1810. Known as the David McKinney Mill, it is on the National Register of Historic Places and part of the Red Mill Museum Village.

(Left) The Ironbound neighborhood in Newark, like so many intercity neighborhoods, has a long history of immigration of peoples from around the world to work in the industries that once thrived here. This Immigrants Memorial Monument, created by sculptor Camilo Satiro and dedicated in 2018, depicts 14 working class people of different races, ages and origins, all of whom built the city and the country as they created a new life for themselves in the city.

(Above) The Bergen County Martin Luther King Jr. Monument stands on the campus of Fairleigh Dickinson University in Hackensack. Unveiled in 2014, the plaques on the wall contain quotes from King's speeches. The monument is intended to encourage leadership skills, excellence and integrity in the student body as well as to commemorate King's legacy.

The USS *New Jersey* was commissioned in 1943 and served until 1991. An Iowa-class battleship, she weighs 50,000 tons, is 887 feet long and her four turbines each produce more than 53,000 horsepower. Nicknamed "Big J," the ship won 19 battle stars and is the most decorated battleship in the history of the United States Navy. When on active duty, the *New Jersey* carried 1,900 officers and crew. Now docked permanently in Camden as a museum, the ship receives over 80,000 visitors a year.

Thomas Edison's house, Glenmont, is located in the gated community of Llewellyn Park, West Orange near the Edison Laboratory Complex. Completed in 1882 for Henry Pedder, Edison bought the house in 1886 for the equivalent of about four million dollars today.

The house retains the original furniture and personal items used by Edison and his family and is a popular museum. It has 29 rooms, central heat, flush toilets and hot and cold running water. Edison added electric light in 1887.

The interior of the Heavy Machine Shop at the Thomas Edison National Historical Park in West Orange is a popular attraction. Most of these tools were installed in 1888 and many are still in working order today.

The Thomas Edison National Historical Park includes more than a dozen buildings that were used by Edison in his research into electricity, photography and motion pictures.

The Stone Pony in Asbury Park opened in 1974 and almost immediately became one of the most important music clubs in the country. Bruce Springsteen is just one of the famous artists who played at the Pony.

(Right) Hurd Park in Dover features a scenic walking trail, oak trees, a stream and several war memorials. The park is famous for its cherry blossoms in the spring.

Asbury Park in Monmouth County is a small beachfront city on the Jersey Shore. Developed in 1871 as a residential resort, the waterfront boardwalk became an instant success and by 1912 the summer population reached several hundred thousand people. The 1920s, a boom time for the Jersey Shore communities, saw the construction of the Paramount Theatre (right), the Casino Arena and the Carousel House (above). Asbury Park's beautiful architecture has survived years of neglect and now, after extensive renovations, the area seems destined to return to its former prominence.

PARAMOUN
1968

Newark, one of the oldest cities in the state, was originally settled in 1666. The downtown core is the state's insurance, legal and technology center. Despite being the largest city in New Jersey, Newark still retains a human scale with many older skyscrapers in active use.

These red brick townhouses with their ornate iron railings are in the Hamilton Park historic area of Jersey City, a much sought after residential section of the city.

Pier C Park along the Hudson River Waterfront Walkway in Hoboken was opened in 2010. Although only a little over an acre in size there are children's playgrounds, seating areas and paths to enjoy. The stunning view across the Hudson River to Manhattan makes Pier C a favorite place to relax in the city.

The Port Newark-Elizabeth Marine Terminal is the most important container ship facility on the East Coast of the United States. As well as facilities to load and unload container ships, the port has extensive repair and maintenance facilities for all sizes of ships.

Ellis Island is owned by the federal government but is located inside the borders of New Jersey and New York states. From 1892 to 1954, more than 12 million people passed through Ellis Island on their way to immigrating into the United States. The island contains the National Museum of Immigration and is part of the Statue of Liberty National Monument. It is only accessible by a ferry that leaves from Liberty State Park in Jersey City. Each year the gates of the Visitor Center (above) welcome more than 3,700,000 people who visit the island.

RCY·BL ARE THE CLEAN OF HEART FOR THEY SHALL SEE GOD BL ARE THE PEACEMAKERS

(Left) The beautiful, traditional interior of St. Michael Roman Catholic Church in Jersey City includes the magnificent stained-glass windows that were added in 1902. Built in 1867, the building has been preserved with restoration projects in 2007, 2012 and 2014.

(Above) This intricate spire crowns the roof of the Cathedral Basilica of the Sacred Heart in Newark. Sacred Heart is the fifth largest cathedral building in North America and is famous for its beautiful, traditional Gothic architecture. Construction began in 1899 but work on the interior was not completed until 1954.

The sand, sun and surf at Ocean City provides the perfect spot for a relaxing summer day at the beach. The boardwalk in the background provides a change for anyone wanting more excitement.

The New Jersey Lottery Festival of Ballooning is held each year at Solberg Airport, Whitehouse Station. Over 100 hot air balloons take part, providing a rainbow of color and an unforgettable show for spectators and participants alike.

Six Flags Great Adventure & Six Flags Wild Safari Adventure in Jackson Township is the second-largest theme park in the world, covering over 500 acres. The El Toro roller coaster (left) is one of the largest wooden roller coasters in the world and reaches speeds of up to 70 miles an hour. A trip through the safari park offers a chance to see lions, tigers, elephants and giraffes just outside the car window.

The Princeton Tigers have played their home games at Powers Field at Princeton Stadium since 1998. The stadium can seat more than 27,000 fans.

These two bronze tigers, a gift to the school from Woodrow Wilson's Class of 1879, guard the entrance to Nassau Hall, Princeton's oldest building, completed in 1756.

DEI SVB NVMINE VIGET
ANNO DOMINI MDCCCXCVI
HAMILTON JEWELERS
HAMILTON
NO STOPPING OR STANDING

(Left) Nassau Street, the shopping heart of Princeton, is directly across the street from the university. Witherspoon Street, once the heart of the Black community in Princeton, was known as "African Lane" in the 19th century. Hamilton Jewelers' mock-Tudor building is a major landmark on the famous street.

(Above) The Mather Sundial in McCosh Courtyard was given to Princeton in 1907 by Sir William Mather. It was a symbol of the connection between Oxford and Princeton Universities, as well as the connection between Great Britain and America.

The Fountain of Freedom, created by James FitzGerald in 1966, is one of the iconic landmarks on the Princeton campus. At 23 feet in height and weighing six tons, it is one of the largest cast bronze sculptures in the United States.

(Left) Blair Arch built in 1897, is one of the most famous examples of Gothic architecture that makes Princeton's campus one of the most beautiful in the country. Known for its acoustics, the arch is used by a cappella groups each year.

Albert Einstein arrived in Princeton in 1933 to work at the Institute for Advanced Study and remained in the city until his death in 1955. This bronze bust was created by Robert Berks and unveiled in 2005.

(Right) The Joseph Henry House in Princeton was built in 1838. The structure has been moved three times and was placed at its present position in 1946. The house was used by the Dean of the College but now houses the Andlinger Center for the Humanities.

JOSEPH HENRY HOUSE
Andlinger Center for the Humanities

Iceboat races have been held annually on the Navesink River in Red Bank for more than a century. Organized by the North Shrewsbury Ice Boat & Yacht Club, the longest active iceboat club in the world. The fastest boats can achieve speeds of up to 100 miles per hour.

Called “The Iron Man” by many, this giant stainless steel sculpture of a hockey player about to take a slapshot was installed at Championship Plaza in front of the Prudential Center in Newark. Created by Jon Krawczyk, a lifelong Devils fan, in 2009, it stands 22 feet tall and weighs 7,000 pounds.

Lucy the Elephant has been a tourist attraction in Margate since 1881. Made of wood and covered in tin, Lucy stands 65 feet tall and was built to promote real estate sales and attract tourists to the area. Today she is the oldest roadside attraction in the United States.

The Margate World War II Memorial Lifeguard Races are held in August. Lifeguards from beaches along the Atlantic Coast compete in a one-mile doubles row, a one-thousand-foot singles row and a half mile swim.

Grounds For Sculpture in Hamilton is a unique museum, sculpture garden, and arboretum. Nearly 300 contemporary sculptures are located outside on 42 acres of parkland, while indoors there are six galleries. Educational programs and hands-on workshops are offered all year.

Water's Soul, created by Jaume Plensa from fiberglass, resin and marble dust, stands on the Hudson River waterfront in the Newport section of Jersey City. The sculpture, approximately 80 feet in height, depicts the head of a young person with eyes closed and a finger pressed against the lips in a pose that asks us to be quiet and take time to appreciate and conserve the precious water around us and recognize its value.

The Old Barracks Museum in Trenton was built in 1758 to house British soldiers but was used by both British and American forces during the Revolutionary War as control of Trenton changed hands.

Battle of Monmouth reenactments are held each year in Monmouth Battlefield State Park, Manalapan to commemorate General George Washington's 1778 attack on British forces that were moving from Philadelphia to New York.

The Boardwalk in Wildwood is one of the last surviving seaside amusement parks on the Atlantic Coast. The first boardwalk was built in the 1890s and was only 150 yards long. Today, the boardwalk stretches for two and a half miles and is packed with more than 100 shops, arcades, waterparks, restaurants, rides and attractions. The action is nonstop and there is always something new to see and do.

AQUARIUM
18 HOLE
GOLF
AQUARIUM
OLD TIME PHOTOS
T-shirt
Time!
Family Clothing Store

This Nike Hercules Missile is one of the exhibits at the Sandy Hook Unit of Gateway National Recreation Area. These missiles were designed to shoot down enemy aircraft and operated out of Fort Hancock until the fort was closed in 1974.

The Naval Air Station Wildwood Aviation Museum is located inside a World War II hangar at the airport in Cape May. The collection of military aircraft is focused on World War II, but also includes aircraft that saw service in Korea and Vietnam.

The Bel Air Motel is one of many buildings featuring Doo Wop architecture in the motel strip in Wildwood. Palm trees, tiki huts, bright neon colors, kidney-shaped swimming pools and outdoor iron balconies evoke the feeling of the classic American beach towns of the 1950s and 1960s, the heyday of automobile vacations.

The Wildwood Boardwalk has been a vacation destination since the 1890s. More than 70,000 wooden planks stretch for 38 blocks to support all the carnival games, shops, restaurants, arcades and more than 100 rides and attractions.

The new Goethals Bridge connects Elizabeth, New Jersey to Staten Island, NY. The eastbound span opened in 2017 and the westbound span a year later. The bridge is over 7,000 feet long, rises more than 140 feet over the water and carries an average of over 90,000 vehicles a day.

(Right) The George Washington Bridge opened in 1931 and has seen much expansion and renovation since then. The 4,700-foot-long double-decked suspension bridge connects Fort Lee with New York City. One of the busiest bridges in the world, it carries over 100 million vehicles a year and is a major link between the states.

This spectacular waterfall in Paterson Great Falls National Historic Park drops 77 feet and is 260 feet wide. It once provided power for early industries in Paterson, the first planned industrial city in the United States. The town was named for Governor William Paterson but was planned and established in large part by Alexander Hamilton (above) who saw the value of the area's abundant water power to attract industries.

(Left) The World War II Memorial overlooking the river in Hoboken commemorates the 159 residents of the city who were killed in the Second World War. The memorial was opened in 2008 close to Pier C Park on the Hudson River.

(Right) This memorial, *To the Struggle Against World Terrorism*, in Bayonne, is dedicated to those killed in the 1993 and 9/11 attacks on the World Trade Center in New York. Commonly called the Tear Drop Memorial, it was a gift from the Russian government in 2005. The 100-foot-high, bronze-clad tower is broken in the middle with a nickel surfaced teardrop hanging in the opening. Plaques on the sides contain the names of those killed in the two terrorist attacks.

COURAGE

The World War II Memorial at Veterans Park was created in 2008 to honor those citizens of New Jersey who served in World War II. Located across the street from the New Jersey State House in Trenton, the monument lists the names of those who received the New Jersey Medal of Honor.

Lady Victory (above) is a symbol that was used to promote the war effort. She represents the sacrifice and dedication of those who served. Murals depict battle scenes in Atlantic and Pacific theaters of war.

Adventure Aquarium, Camden (right) contains over two million gallons of water and houses 8,000 animals in fresh and salt water habitats. There is a tropical waterfall tank, a shark tank, a kid's zone, African penguins, stingrays, turtles and many other forms of aquatic and semi-aquatic life. It was voted the best aquarium on the East Coast by *USA Today* in 2024.

URE
AQUARIUM

The BAPS Swaminarayan Akshardham in Robbinsville is the largest Hindu mandir (Hindu house of worship) in the United States and the second-largest in the world. Designed in accordance with ancient Hindu scriptures, the temple features elements from Hindu heritage and is 191 feet high, 255 feet wide, and 345 feet long and sits on 185 acres. Elephants are sacred symbols that represent the virtues of loyalty, strength, wisdom and fertility. These statues (right) stand outside the mandir.

MetLife Stadium is a multi-purpose event location in the Meadowlands Sports Complex in East Rutherford. The stadium, which seats 82,500 people, is home to the New York Giants and the New York Jets of the National Football League. MetLife Stadium opened in 2010 and replaced the old Giants Stadium. Unlike many modern stadiums, it does not have a retractable roof.

(Right) Monmouth Park Racetrack, in Oceanport, has a long history dating back to 1870. The main track is a one-mile dirt oval with provisions for one-and-a-quarter mile races and a turf course. The racetrack also features trackside sportsbook betting, luxury restaurants and a miniature golf course. Monmouth receives over half a million visitors a year.

(Right) This traditional red barn and outbuildings stand out against the snow at Hidden Spring Lavender Farm in Skillman. The rural character of much of the state continues, despite its thriving cities and coastline. Many old barns like this one (above) have been abandoned and are slowly collapsing back into the soil but still retain a presence of the agriculture heritage of the state.

This monument in Haddonfield commemorates the discovery of 35 large bones in a field outside the town in 1858. The bones proved to be from *Hadrosaurus foulkii*, a dinosaur about 25 feet long that weighed 7–8 tons and lived more than 70–80 million years ago. The bones were assembled and put on display at the Academy of Natural Sciences in Philadelphia in 1868. The site is now a National Historic Landmark and *Hadrosaurus foulkii* has been designated the official dinosaur of New Jersey. The statue is at the intersection of Kings Highway East and Lantern Lane in downtown Haddonfield.

Historic Cold Spring Village contains many well-preserved historic buildings and is located in Cape May. There are over 20 buildings on a 30-acre site that features interpreters and guides in period dress. The village is open from June to September. The pillory was used for punishment. Offenders would have their head and arms inserted and would then be the subject of taunts and shame.

(Above) The Katyń Memorial at Exchange Place, Jersey City is dedicated to the memory of the thousands of Polish army officers and civic leaders who were murdered in March and April 1940 after the Soviet invasion of Poland. The 34-foot-tall memorial depicts a Polish soldier with a rifle bayonet in his back.

Jersey City's beautiful waterfront at the Exchange Place development has enticed so many financial service businesses to relocate here that the area has been nicknamed Wall Street West. Jersey City is the second largest city in the state by population. It's proximity to New York and the extensive redevelopment of the waterfront has attracted many residents.

The New Jersey Pine Barrens is the largest of the pine barrens on the Atlantic Coast. These areas are called "barrens" because the sandy, acidic soil made it impossible for the early settlers to grow food crops. To protect the area as a wild land, congress created the New Jersey Pinelands National Reserve in 1978 giving protection to over one million acres. Although mostly covered in pine forest, many areas have water (right) and extensive, almost tropical growth.

Batsto Village is located in Wharton State Forest, which is part of the Pinelands National Reserve. The name derives from a Swedish word meaning bathing place. A blast furnace was built on the site by 1766 and the iron works were run until the middle of the 1800s.

The property was acquired by the state in the mid-1950s and work started on the restoration of the buildings on the property. There are now more than 40 restored structures, including the mansion (right) and the village is one of the most popular tourist attractions in New Jersey.

This young seal is basking in the sun on Long Beach Island, a destination equally popular with human tourists. The island is about 18 miles long but only one-half mile at its widest. It is accessed by a single causeway and is home to about 10,000 year-round residents but during peak summer holiday season the population can swell to over 100,000.

PHOTO CREDITS

ALAMY

Panther Media GmbH: 2; Jerry Fornarotto: 12; Jerry Fornarotto: 15; sep120 / Stockimo: 18; Jerry Fornarotto: 24; Robert K. Chin: 26; Jon Arnold Images Ltd: 27; Robert K. Chin: 28; Robert K. Chin: 29; Diane Modafferi: 30; Wayne Bruzek: 32; travelstock44: 38; Clarence Holmes Photography: 40; Hilda DeSanctis: 47; Sandra Baker: 49; Jon Bilous: 50; Randy Duchaine: 52; Bill Crnkovich: 56; Laperruque: 58; Philip Scalia: 63; MIHAI ANDRITOIU: 68; J. Schwanke: 69; Renate Strub: 70; Tom Cassidy: 72; Joe Benning: 81; Mira: 89; Tom Till: 91; Tom Reichner: 93

SHUTTERSTOCK

Mihai_Andritoiu: cover; Dennis MacDonald: 6; Alizada Studios: 7; Mihai_Andritoiu: 8–9; Mihai_Andritoiu: 10–11; Alizada Studios: 13; Andrew F. Kazmierski: 14; Mihai_Andritoiu: 16–17; Wangkun Jia: 19; ARK NEYMAN: 20; Bryan Little: 21; Alysson M: 22; quiggyt4: 23; Eric Dale: 25; George Wirt: 31; George Wirt: 33; Leonid Andronov: 34; James Andrews1: 35; Mihai_Andritoiu: 36; Roman Babakin: 37; Zack Frank: 39; Felix Lipov: 41; Gary C. Tognoni: 42; Ancesc: 43; Pit Stock: 44; JaysonPhotography: 45; Helen89: 46; Benjamin Clapp: 48; Jay Yuan: 51; Oleg Kovtun Hydrobio: 53; James Kirkikis: 54; Alysson M: 55; Dominick Corrado: 57; 365 Focus Photography: 59; Jeffrey M. Frank: 60; Andrew F. Kazmierski: 61; Rosemarie Mosteller: 62; EQRoy: 64; EQRoy: 65; EQRoy: 66; James Kirkikis: 67; EQRoy: 71; ARK NEYMAN: 73; quiggyt4: 74; Felix Lipov: 75; Oleg Kovtun Hydrobio: 76; Serge Yatunin: 78; Photo Spirit: 79; George Wirt: 80; EQRoy: 82; Linda Harms: 83; EQRoy: 84; Jeffrey M. Frank: 85; Sean Pavone: 86; ARK NEYMAN: 87; quiggyt4: 88; Patrick Tappe: 90; Michael Moloney: 92; Mariusz Lopusiewicz: 96

WIKIMEDIA COMMONS

Ajay_suresh: 77

INDEX

Monument to Frank Sinatra on the waterfront
in Hoboken.